MAR '92 JUNIOR

DATE DUE			
APR 30 '92			
MAR 1 4 '94			
MAR 1 0 '95			
APR 1 8 '95			
MAR 25 '97			
AR 1 1 '98			
MAY 18 '99			
MAY 09 '01			
DEC 2 6 '01			

GLORIA STEINEM
The Women's Movement

by
Mark Hoff

New Directions
The Millbrook Press
Brookfield, Connecticut

Produced in Association with Agincourt Press.
Interior Design: Tilman Reitzle

Photographs courtesy of: AP/Wide World Photos: 6, 25, 27, 38, 58, 72, 82; *People*: 9; Washington Star Photograph Collection (copyright Washington Post; reprinted by permission of the Washington, D.C. Public Library): 17, 53, 65; Smith College: 22; The Bettmann Archive: 34; Sophia Smith collection, Smith College: 45; Michael Ochs Archives, Venice, CA: 85.

Cataloging-in-Publication Data

Hoff, Mark.
Gloria Steinem: the women's movement.

100 p.; ill.: (New directions)
Bibliography: p.
Includes index.

Summary: A biography of feminist leader Gloria Steinem, emphasizing her role in the women's liberation movement of the 1970s.
1. Steinem, Gloria, 1934–   . 2. Women—Civil Rights.
3. Equal rights amendments. I. Title. II. Series.

B (92)
ISBN 1-878841-19-X

Contents

Introduction

This book tells the life story of an intriguing woman— Gloria Steinem. But it is also about the women's movement of the 1960s and 1970s, which Steinem helped lead.

In 1963, Betty Friedan wrote a book called *The Feminine Mystique,* which became a rallying cry in the battle for women's rights. In its pages, Friedan exposed the ways in which society discriminated against women. In the years that followed, the women's movement grew in both size and influence, and Gloria Steinem was very much at the heart of it. During this time, women found that they shared many problems, such as barriers to abortion, physical abuse, and lack of political and economic influence.

Some women began to work together to solve their common problems. They pressured politicians, organized political protests, and founded the National Organization of Women to develop and promote their cause. If the feminist movement was to educate people, however, it had to communicate with them first. Gloria Steinem's major accomplishment was to place the women's movement in the national spotlight. Her skills as a writer made her a good teacher, and her knowledge of magazine publishing made possible the founding of *Ms.,* a publication that reached a wide national audience.

Gloria Steinem's work was not easy, and there is still much to be done. But because she and her colleagues fought on, women today have a greater chance for equality.

Eric Hirsch
Assistant Professor of Sociology
Providence College

Steinem at her typewriter.

1

A March and a Movement

The day was July 9, 1978. The crowds had been gathering since early morning. They came by car, by bus, by plane, and on foot to Washington, D.C., for the historic Women's March on Washington. Many were dressed in white to honor the first American women who had fought for the right to vote, and as the march began they became a vibrant wave of white that swept down the wide avenues of the nation's capital. The flags, hand-lettered signs, and banners the marchers carried fluttered in the breeze.

Walking proudly at the head of the march, surrounded by other leaders of the women's movement, was the unmistakable figure of Gloria Steinem. With the long, blond-streaked hair and aviator glasses that had become her trademarks, Steinem was the picture of a charismatic leader, and she led the march with the confidence of a woman who knew exactly what her cause meant. Equality for women was an ideal for which countless Americans had struggled. The march that Steinem led followed in the long and distinquished tradition of Americans fighting for democratic ideals.

The specific goal of the Women's March on Washington was to persuade Congress to grant an extension of the deadline for passage of the Equal Rights Amendment (ERA). This amendment would guarantee equal treatment under the law to all men and women in the United

States. Gloria Steinem and other leaders of the women's movement had planned the march to show support for passage of the ERA. But they also wanted to prove to the government once and for all that women's issues were very important to the American voters, regardless of their race or sex.

The Women's March on Washington was a grass-roots event that recalled the civil rights marches of the 1960s because it united women and men from many races and social classes. Planners of the march had hoped to draw about twenty-five thousand demonstrators. By the end of the day, however, newspaper estimates placed the number at closer to one hundred thousand, exceeding even the wildest expectations. It was the largest gathering for the cause of equal rights for women in the nation's history.

Several hours into the march, Steinem stepped up to the speaker's platform and addressed the huge crowd of supporters. She spoke of the historic purpose of the march and of the women's movement behind it that had created a revolution in American society.

The course that had brought Gloria Steinem to the leadership of that march and that movement had not been an easy one. She had endured great poverty and family tragedy as a child and had spent her teen years in a lonely, rat-infested house with a mother who suffered from mental illness. One of her few pleasures had been taking tap-dancing lessons, and she had dreamed of becoming an entertainer. But later, her aspirations changed and she decided instead to go to college and become a journalist, following in the footsteps of her mother.

Through persistence and great dedication, Steinem fulfilled those ambitions and then went on to even greater things. After graduating *magna cum laude* from Smith College in 1956, she worked hard as a journalist, and, defying discrimination, earned the right to write serious articles on important political issues of her time. Finally, she became a political figure herself, a celebrity in fact, and a symbol of a new era.

On speaking tours throughout the United States, Gloria Steinem has addressed sold-out halls and audi-toriums in places as disparate as San Francisco, California, and Wichita, Kansas. She has appeared on the covers of *Newsweek, McCall's,* and *People* magazines. Her face has become a familiar sight in the nation's leading newspapers and on television. Always controversial and always challenging the status quo, Steinem has in-fluenced the opinions of several generations of American women—and men. In doing so, she has become one of the most recognizable symbols of the feminist movement in the United States.

On the cover of
People *magazine.*

2

A Difficult Childhood

Gloria Steinem's parents announced her birth on March 25, 1934, with a special card sent to their friends. It read "Gloria Marie Steinem—8½ Pound Blues Singer—World Premier Appearance." The message was unusual but so, it turned out, were the first years of Steinem's life. The Steinems had not really expected her to become a blues singer, but her father had a playful sense of humor. His unique announcement of his daughter's birth hinted that Gloria Steinem's life would also be unconventional. He was more prophetic than he realized.

Gloria was the second of two daughters born to Leo and Ruth Nuneviller Steinem. Leo Steinem was a free-spirited man who prided himself on his ability to remain independent. For many years, he supported the family with an antiques business that took the Steinems all over the country, as Leo bought and sold antiques.

Gloria's mother was an intelligent, capable woman who had graduated from Oberlin College in Ohio. In her youth, she had pursued a career in journalism and achieved considerable success. However, against the wishes of her family, she gave up her career when she married Leo Steinem.

Gloria's early childhood was spent traveling from one state to another in the family's crowded house trailer. At first, she had the company of her sister Susanne, who was ten years older. But around the time when Gloria turned eight, Susanne went away to college in Massachusetts.

During the winter months, the Steinems usually travelled to the warmer states, such as Florida or California. But because they rarely stayed in one place for very long, Gloria did not attend school regularly. This also meant that she didn't have a chance to make many friends her own age.

As a result, Gloria enjoyed the summer months best, when the Steinem family stayed at a resort colony in Clark Lake, Michigan. During the summers, Leo Steinem would manage Ocean Beach Pier, an entertainment hall that he owned there. Steinem's establishment presented music and dance programs for vacationing families. It was there that Gloria first took tap dancing lessons and first dreamed of becoming a performer. She also made friends, many of whom were jazz musicians and dancers working at the resort.

Eventually, though, Leo Steinem closed the business in Michigan when it began to lose money. The Steinem family had never been well off, but when the hall closed they fell on very hard times. Things got so bad that Leo Steinem feared he would be unable to support the family. Soon it was decided that he would go to California to pursue his antiques business, while the rest of the family remained in the East. It was a great shock to Gloria when she found out that the family would split up.

Susanne had to return to college in Massachusetts, so Gloria and her mother moved with her to Amherst. They lived there for one year and then moved again to Toledo, Ohio. Finally, Gloria began attending school regularly.

Living with her mother in Toledo was extremely difficult for Gloria because Ruth Steinem had frequent bouts of severe depression and anxiety. Gloria had long been aware of her mother's mental illness, of course, but in the past she had had her father with her. Now she was living alone with her mother, so she learned much more about her mother and the origin of Ruth's psychological problems.

Leo Steinem's unconventional life had been very difficult for Ruth. She had felt extremely lonely during the times when Leo travelled in search of antiques for his business. And this loneliness, combined with the disappointment of having to give up her job as a reporter, may have contributed to the mental illness that followed.

Several years before Gloria was born, when Susanne was only five years old, Ruth Steinem had suffered a nervous breakdown. She had spent several months in a sanatorium, a special residence for mentally ill people, then recovered enough to come home and work at the Clark Lake resort. During Gloria's childhood, however, her mother regularly took tranquilizers to control her anxiety.

Living with her mother in Toledo, Gloria quickly learned just how powerful her mother's medicine could be. Often Ruth's speech would be slurred, leading neighbors and school friends to think she was drunk. Many times, Gloria had to prepare their meals, shop for food, and keep the house in order, with little or no help from her mother.

Sometimes Gloria wished that her mother would stop taking her medicine. However, she soon learned the effects of not taking the medicine. Without medicine,

Ruth had great trouble sleeping. One terrible night, when Ruth had stopped taking her medicine and had gone without sleep for several days, she pushed her hand through a window. When Gloria rushed into the room, she saw with horror that her mother's arm was covered with blood. After that, Gloria saw to it that her mother took her medicine regularly.

Incidents such as this took their toll on Gloria. She had to watch her mother constantly, always remaining fearful that something horrible would happen again. This meant that Gloria did not have much time to be with friends. She was also self-conscious about her mother's condition and the poverty in which they lived. In an autobiographical account published in 1984, Steinem described her childhood life with her mother:

> She was just a fact of life when I was growing up; someone to be worried about and cared for; an invalid who lay in bed with eyes closed and lips moving in occasional response to voices only she could hear; a woman to whom I brought an endless stream of toast and coffee, bologna sandwiches and dime pies, in a child's version of what meals should be.[1]

When things were unusually difficult, Gloria even imagined that Ruth was not her real mother. Instead she imagined that she had been adopted, and that one day her real parents would come to rescue her. One of her few means of escape at this time was going to the movies with her friends. Watching the movies sometimes led her to daydream about becoming a Hollywood movie star.

Another way that Gloria escaped from her troubles was by reading. She read everything—novels, mystery stories, philosophy, books about horses and dancing. Her favorite writer was Louisa May Alcott, the author of *Little Women*. She also came to depend on her hobbies, such as tap dancing, to control some of the instability in her life. Sometimes she even taught classes to pay for her own lessons, and she also earned pocket money by performing at the Toledo Eagles Club and local school shows.

From California, Gloria's father tried to send money home, but times were often difficult for him as well. Sometimes he was not able to send any money, and Gloria and her mother had to make do with very little. Fortunately, they earned a small income by renting the downstairs apartment in their house.

Yet Gloria's life in Toledo with her mother was not always troubled. When her mother was well, they would share happy times, talking of their dreams for the future. Sometimes they would receive visits from Gloria's uncle or her aunts. Once Gloria's mother took her to an audition for an amateur acting group, and when Gloria got a part in a Biblical drama, her mother helped produce the play.

At about this time, Gloria learned about her family's history from her mother. She learned that both Leo and Ruth's parents had disapproved of their marriage. Leo was Jewish, while Ruth was Protestant. Her mother also taught her about her father's Jewish heritage, and the great suffering that Jews in Europe had undergone during the Holocaust.

A crisis in Gloria's life came during her junior year in high school, when Ruth became severely depressed. Gloria did not know what to do to help her, and the family did not have the money to seek expensive medical help. In addition, Gloria had terrible memories of an earlier visit to a doctor, who had recommended that Ruth be put in an institution for the mentally ill. Gloria had strongly disagreed. She had felt that her mother's condition would never improve within the confines of a mental hospital.

In those days, mental health problems were not as well understood as they are today. The most common treatment for mental illnesses then was to put patients in special institutions. In Gloria's family, too, mental illness was not well understood. Some relatives blamed Ruth for her own illness and believed that she could change if she really wanted to.

Many years later, Gloria Steinem came to understand her mother's mental illness in terms of the struggles and frustrations of her life. She also related her mother's terrible difficulties to the problems of women everywhere who receive little sympathy if they become weak or sick. Having witnessed her mother's suffering firsthand, Steinem spoke out strongly against what she saw as prejudice against women. Many people, she argued, tended to see the illnesses of women in terms of personal failings, personality disorders, or character flaws, while similar problems in men were often explained by referring to problems in a man's working life. Steinem pointed out this double standard when describing her mother's condition:

> Even the explanation of mental illness seemed to contain more personal fault when applied to my mother. She had suffered her first "nervous break-

15

down," as she and everyone else called it, before I was born and when my sister was about five. It followed years of trying to take care of a baby, be the wife of a kind but financially irresponsible man with show-business dreams, and still keep her much-loved job as reporter and newspaper editor. After many months in a sanatorium, she was pronounced recovered. That is, she was able to take care of my sister again, to move away from the city and the job she loved, and to work with my father at the isolated rural lake in Michigan he was trying to transform into a resort worthy of the big dance bands of the 1930s.[2]

As Ruth's condition worsened, new misfortunes struck the Steinems. Because the house had fallen into considerable disrepair over the years, rats from abandoned buildings nearby began to run through the rooms. Gloria would sometimes wake up at night and pull her toes beneath the covers because she was afraid they might be bitten off by rats. The furnace also broke down. She did not know how they would live through another winter.

As Gloria neared graduation from high school, she was unsure of her future. She wanted to go to college but was afraid to leave her mother on her own. She tried to talk to her sister about her problems, but Susanne could not help her very much. The future did not look bright.

Yet just when things appeared to be at their worst, a ray of hope came into Gloria's life. The church next door offered to buy the Steinem's house. When Susanne learned of the offer, she suggested a plan. By telephone,

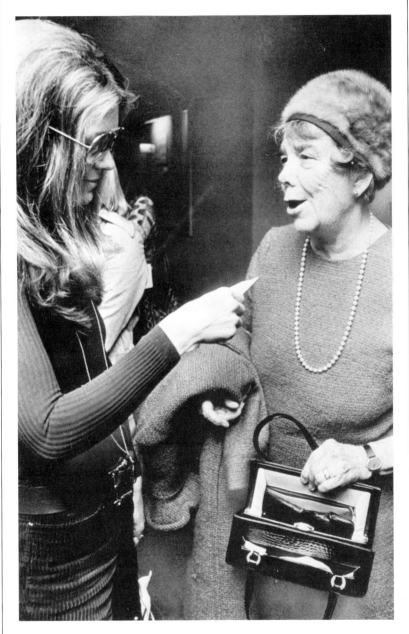

With her mother, Ruth Nuneviller Steinem.

she proposed that their father Leo take care of their mother, while Gloria came to live with Susanne in Washington, D.C., where she would finish her senior year of high school and then go on to college.

Gloria responded that their father would never agree to such a plan. She knew well how difficult it would be for him to care for Ruth while he carried on his antiques business. Nevertheless, Susanne scheduled a family conference in Toledo. During the summer of 1951, Gloria, Susanne, and their father sat down to discuss the future.

Susanne explained the plan. They would sell the house, and the money from the sale would then enable Leo to take care of Ruth and free Gloria to move to Washington. But Leo refused, explaining that it was impossible for him to care for Ruth while travelling on business. Gloria understood her father's difficulties, yet her heart sank. Her only hope was gone.

Later that day, Leo drove Gloria to the store where she had a summer job. As she was about to get out of the car, she suddenly burst into tears. Her father was shocked at her grief.

And then Gloria felt Leo's arms around her, comforting her. He explained that he would agree to take care of Ruth for one year, but only one year. Gloria's heart soared in happiness. A year seemed like an eternity. For the first time, she would have a chance to lead the life she had dreamed about—the normal life of a high school girl.

3

A New Beginning

Once Gloria moved to Washington, the difference was immediate. She enrolled at Western High School for her senior year and worked hard there. Outside the classroom, she had a full social life and proved to be very popular. She was even elected vice-president of her class.

Gloria missed her mother very much, but she was also relieved not to be burdened with the task of caring for her. As a result, she began to think about her mother's life with greater objectivity. She later described the experience of realizing how unhappy her mother's life must have been:

> Pity takes distance and a certainty of surviving. It was only after our house was bought for demolition by the church next door, and after my sister had performed the miracle of persuading my father to give me a carefree time before college by taking my mother with him to California for a year, that I could afford to think about the sadness of her life.[1]

As much as she enjoyed her senior year in high school, Gloria remained worried about her future. She had dreamed of going to college, but always there had been the uncertainty of her mother's condition and the problem of the family's poverty. Now that the house in

Toledo had been sold, however, the family decided that some of the money could be used to pay her tuition. Susanne also agreed to care for their mother while Gloria was away at school.

Steinem set her sights on Smith College in Northampton, Massachusetts. She knew about Smith because Susanne had studied there. Smith was one of the best women's colleges in the country. The competition to get in was tough, which worried Steinem because her high-school grades were not as good as she had wished. However, on the strength of her entrance examinations and the strong recommendation of a high-school adviser, Steinem was accepted. She entered Smith College in the fall of 1952.

In the 1950s, it was by no means taken for granted that a woman would go to college. Most women were expected to get married soon after graduating from high school. Their lives were expected to focus on their husbands and children. College and careers were options not even considered by many young women. But Gloria's mother and sister had both had college educations, and she was expected to follow in their path.

Steinem proved to be an excellent student at Smith, winning several awards and academic honors. She majored in government, a subject she had become deeply interested in during the summer after her graduation from high school, when she had worked as a volunteer for Adlai Stevenson, the Democratic presidential candidate. Steinem had helped publicize his campaign by writing a student newsletter about him.

During Steinem's first semester at Smith, the presidential campaign interested almost everyone. The former general and war hero Dwight D. Eisenhower was the Republican candidate. Steinem observed the political views of her classmates and professors and discovered, to her surprise, that most students preferred Eisenhower, the more conservative candidate, while most professors preferred the more liberal Stevenson. (Conservative politicians generally hold the view that government should play a limited role in solving society's problems. Liberal politicians argue that governments should actively attempt to solve such problems as poverty, lack of education, and inequality among various social groups.)

Steinem later explored this difference between Smith students and professors when she wrote an article about patterns in political movements. In the article, Steinem argued against the prevailing view that young people were generally more liberal than older people, and that people tended to get more conservative as they grew older. She wrote that the opposite was true—that people actually tended to become more liberal as they grew older and gained more experience. This was especially true for women, she wrote.

At Smith, Steinem was also exposed to many new influences. It did not take her long, for example, to discover that many of her classmates came from wealthy families who favored their children with large monthly allowances. But this did not bother Steinem—she considered herself lucky merely to be enrolled at Smith. She was also determined to remain independent, even if that meant she would have to do without many of the possessions that her classmates had. Ironically, Steinem later discovered that some of her friends envied her for her independence.

Perhaps even more important, however, was Steinem's realization that she had an unlikely advantage over most of her classmates. She discovered that her background, which she had always considered a handicap, was in some ways advantageous. While Steinem could study and read with great concentration, she found that many of her classmates, who had not endured the years of difficulty and suffering that she had, could not discipline themselves to the same degree. Steinem had learned just how bad things could be in life, and this knowledge made her strong. She resolved that she would improve her life in spite of any obstacles that might be put in her path.

College brought other opportunities as well, such as the chance to study abroad. Smith had an arrangement with the University of Geneva in Switzerland. Steinem, who had studied French, jumped at the chance to put her knowledge of the language to use. In Geneva for her junior year, she studied French, history, and government, and lived with a Swiss family.

Steinem's senior year back at Smith was full of achievements. She was elected to Phi Beta Kappa, an

Smith College

honor society that admits members on the basis of scholastic excellence; she was a candidate for honors in her major, government; and she was chosen senior class historian.

Yet the greatest challenge facing Steinem was figuring out what to do next. Many of her classmates planned to get married and raise families immediately after graduation. She also thought about this alternative—she had a boyfriend to whom she was engaged, Blair Chotzinoff. Steinem had met Chotzinoff on a blind date in New York. He was a former reporter for the *New York Post*, and was so taken with Steinem that he used to rent planes and pilot them to Massachusetts to visit her on weekends. He once described in an interview how he flew over her dormitory and wrote her name in the sky.

Steinem's relationship with Chotzinoff was exciting, but she felt strongly that she did not want to get married right away. She wanted instead to develop her own talents and skills.

Some of the uncertainty about the future cleared up when one of Steinem's professors suggested that she apply for a special scholarship to study in Asia. Chester Bowles, the ambassador to India under President Eisenhower, had established a fellowship at Smith for a student to study in that country. Steinem applied for and won the fellowship.

The Smith College graduation on June 3, 1956, was a proud day for Steinem and her family. Her mother, father, and sister were all there to celebrate this important milestone in her life. It was typical of Steinem, however, that even as she celebrated one achievement, she looked forward to yet another adventure.

4

The Writer Emerges

The hot, muggy night air and exotic sounds of the Indian city of Bombay enveloped Gloria Steinem as she stepped down from the airplane onto the soft black tarmac. She knew at once that her life there would be unlike anything she had ever known before.

Bombay was a dynamic city, the bustling business and entertainment center of India. Steinem saw fascinating sights on the streets. She was amazed by the incredible numbers of people—thousands riding bicycles, packed into buses, or walking with colorful bundles, selling food and other wares.

Several days later, she travelled to New Delhi, India's capital, and enrolled with another student from Smith at Delhi University. They lived in a dormitory in a women's college near the university. Steinem and her classmate were the first American students to live in the college's dormitories.

At this point in her life, Steinem still did not know exactly what she wanted to do professionally. She had decided, however, that she wanted her work to make a humanitarian contribution to the world. Her classes in government, as well as her work for Adlai Stevenson, had influenced her choice.

India, it turned out, would be an excellent place for Steinem to begin. In 1957, just ten years after it had won independence from Britain, India was still an extremely

New Delhi in the 1950s.

poor nation—much poorer than it is today. At that time the country could not feed much of its population, but Indians were working to improve food production by introducing new farming methods. Steinem felt inspired by India's ambitious plans for the future.

At the university, Steinem studied history and government. She was often called upon to defend American foreign policy to Indian students, who were sometimes critical of American politics. At other times, though, she was asked to explain how people lived in the United States. Indians were especially curious about a practice that did not exist in India: dating. Sometimes the Indian students asked Steinem and her friend to perform American songs and dances, and in return they performed Indian songs and dances for the American students.

Steinem was encouraged to follow Indian customs while living in India, and she occasionally wore Indian clothes. Indian women wore saris, which consist of a long piece of fabric wound around the waist and draped over one shoulder. Steinem was also invited to attend traditional Indian ceremonies, which she enjoyed very much.

Steinem also enjoyed wandering through the narrow streets of New Delhi, watching the people working at their jobs, observing the sights at the public market, and breathing in the pungent smells of Indian spices and Indian cooking.

She discovered that most Indians lived in extremely poor conditions. Many homes were in tiny villages that lacked the comforts most Americans took for granted. In the cities people slept in the streets and wore rags. Steinem also learned that most Indians did not own any land, even those who farmed to support themselves. Instead, a few wealthy people owned a large proportion of the land and forced poor people to pay rent to farm it. This knowledge made Steinem feel guilty about her living conditions, which were luxurious by comparison.

Soon she decided to join with a group of Indians who were concerned about the problem of land ownership. She had heard of a man named Vinoba Bhave, who was leading a movement to redistribute the land so that poor Indians would be able to own more of it.

The great Indian independence leader Mohandas Gandhi had begun the Indian tradition of leading marches throughout the land to protest specific policies of India's colonial British rulers. Bhave's plan was to follow in Gandhi's footsteps, walking across India to draw attention to his cause. The marchers were to take

Vinoba Bhave marching across India.

nothing along but the clothing they wore and a bowl with which to ask for food. Steinem was encouraged to join the group because some of Bhave's followers believed that the presence of a woman would make other women more enthusiastic about taking part.

Week after week, Steinem accompanied the group on their walk across India. During this time, Bhave held many meetings with landlords. He pleaded with them to listen to his ideas and encouraged them to donate some of their holdings to landless Indians. Eventually, such marches by Bhave and his followers would yield over four million acres of land as gifts from wealthy land-owners to India's poor.

This early experience in political action taught Steinem many important lessons. She learned, for in-stance, what commitment to a political cause could achieve. Later in her career, when she sponsored and led protests to advance the cause of the women's movement, she would often remember the lessons of her experiences in India.

Steinem remained in India for two years. Toward the end of her stay, she was asked by the Indian government to write a guidebook that would encourage American students and teachers to visit India. She wrote *The Thousand Indias* and also published several freelance articles in Indian newspapers.

When Steinem returned to the United States in 1958, she was more convinced than ever that she wanted to be involved in political causes that would help people. She had become more conscious of politics and of the ways in which developing nations such as India were trying to modernize their countries and raise living standards.

Having decided that she wanted to be a writer, she first went to New York City, a center of book and magazine publishing that attracted many people who wanted to build careers as writers and editors. On the way she visited her family in Washington. She was glad to see that her mother had received treatment for her illness and was much better. Steinem's sister Susanne had married and was tending to a growing family at this time, and her father was also well.

Coming home was exciting for Steinem, but there were many frustrations as well. People at Smith College were interested in what she had learned in India, and she was asked to speak at the college about her experiences there. However, most people Steinem met were not very interested in a country as distant and unfamiliar as India.

In New York, Steinem searched for work but had little success. In 1958 there were very few women journalists, and those women who did find work were rarely assigned to the types of stories that Steinem was interested in—political stories.

Steinem finally found a job in Cambridge, Massachusetts, working for an organization called the Independent Research Service. This group helped American students travel to Communist youth festivals to discuss democracy. Steinem's job involved talking with students, running the organization's office, and writing educational materials. She was eventually assigned to travel to the Helsinki Youth Festival, where she organized a service that supplied information about democracy to foreign journalists. Much of her work at the Helsinki festival involved talking with journalists, diplomats, and other participants.

Years after Steinem had finished her work with the Independent Research Service, it became known that the organization had been funded by the Central Intelligence Agency (CIA). The fact that the CIA was secretly behind the project angered many people who were critical of CIA policy. These same people accused Steinem of having been an agent for the CIA. Steinem, however, flatly denied the charge, and defended the work the Independent Research Service had done in championing democratic ideals.

Still determined to become a journalist, Steinem returned to New York in 1960 and again began looking for a job as a writer. She moved into a small Manhattan apartment on Fifty-Sixth Street. Her roommate, Barbara Nessim, was a painter whom Steinem had met through work. The two friends divided the apartment in half and set up their belongings. On one side, there were Barbara's painting supplies; on the other, Steinem's desk, type-writer, books, and papers.

Steinem was persistent in her search and eventually found a job working for a small political satire magazine called *Help!* The editor was a cartoonist named Harvey Kurtzman, who had been one of the creators of the famous humor magazine *Mad.* Steinem's job involved contacting celebrities and persuading them to appear on the cover of *Help!* She was a capable employee, but even Kurtzman was surprised by Steinem's ability to charm the important people who later appeared in the magazine. As Kurtzman described Steinem in a 1983 interview in the *Washington Post,*

> She would just pick up the phone and talk to people, and charm them out of the trees. . . . I was probably in love with her back then, just like everyone else.[1]

If Kurtzman was surprised at Steinem's success, she herself was not. Her travels and the years she had spent with entertainers at her father's resort had taught her a great deal about meeting people and persuading them to talk about themselves.

Kurtzman soon introduced Steinem to his friends and acquaintances, and she began to be invited to society parties where she met many famous women and men, many in the worlds of publishing and journalism. These contacts helped her greatly. Soon she found herself involved in the busy social life of New York.

Around this time, Steinem also became friendly with the economist John Kenneth Galbraith, whom she had met through his wife, a graduate of Smith College. President John F. Kennedy had recently appointed Galbraith Ambassador to India, so the Harvard professor was very interested in hearing of Steinem's experiences there. In return, he taught her a great deal about economics, a subject in which she had become quite interested.

Steinem had not been in New York very long before she met Bob Benton, the art director of *Esquire* magazine. Benton introduced her to many writers and editors at the magazine. Steinem grew familiar with the way a magazine operated, and soon she began to write uncredited articles for *Esquire.* Her relationship with Benton grew closer. The pair soon began spending much time together, and even began talking of marriage.

Steinem, however, still felt that she was not ready to marry. Her career was just beginning. Also, in the 1960s, attitudes about relationships were changing. Steinem agreed with the idea of women making their own choices about their professional and personal lives.

Steinem's relationship with Benton was based on this new understanding. Both knew that she would not subordinate her career and personal ambitions to his and that they would continue to have a relationship based on equality. She eventually decided not to marry Benton, and they went their separate ways while remaining friends.

For the most part, the early 1960s were a happy period in Steinem's life. Yet there were bad times as well. Leo Steinem died suddenly in an automobile accident in California in 1962. Despite all the difficulties and hard times that the family had endured, Steinem had adored her father. His death caused her to reflect on all the ways in which he had influenced her life.

Leo Steinem had been a man who valued his independence, refused to be tied to an office job, and who had faced uncertainty and hard times with courage and good humor. His daughter, too, would have cause to use these gifts, realizing that she was very much her father's daughter.

By the early 1960s, Gloria Steinem had begun to achieve the success that she had long sought as a professional writer. She wrote articles for a wide array of magazines and became better known in publishing circles. Then, in 1962, her big break came: She received her first byline when her name was printed above one of the articles she wrote for *Esquire*. The article was about the new choices that confronted young women, who had to plan their futures in a time when expectations about their roles in society were changing. *Esquire* was a magazine directed at a primarily male readership, but Steinem's article addressed issues that were equally important to men and women.

Still, Steinem was not yet given the opportunity to do the sort of reporting she craved. Instead, as it turned out, the assignment that did bring her a measure of fame and success began as something of a joke and was a far cry from the political reporting that was her ambition.

5

From Playboy to Politics

Steinem's 1963 "I Was a Playboy Bunny" article caused a great sensation. The Playboy Club in New York was a popular nightclub owned by Hugh Hefner, the founder of *Playboy* magazine. It was famous for its beautiful young waitresses, known as Bunnies. *Show,* a magazine specializing in humorous articles about New York life, suggested that Steinem get a job as a Bunny in the Playboy Club and write an article about her experiences.

Armed with the invented name and personal history of Marie Catherine Ochs, Steinem appeared at the offices of the Playboy Club and applied for a job. The Playboy advertisement had asked for women who were "pretty and personable" and between 21 and 24 years of age. Steinem was past the age limit, but no one questioned her about it at the club. After a series of interviews and fittings for the tightest outfit she had ever worn, Steinem got the job. She squeezed herself into the Bunny costume and began working at the Playboy Club.

Steinem spent about three weeks as a Bunny. It proved to be far more demanding than she had expected. The job was advertised as exciting and a potential stepping stone to other opportunities, such as roles in movies. Instead, Steinem discovered that the Bunnies had to work long hours under difficult conditions. The Bunnies' tight costumes left marks on their skin, and their three-inch heels often left their feet aching and blistered. Steinem

"I Was a Playboy Bunny."

wrote that her feet were permanently enlarged by a half size from carrying heavy trays while wearing the tight shoes.The pay also proved to be far less than the large sums promised by the club.

Steinem's article was a witty chronicle of the absurd situations and poor working conditions at the Playboy Club, and it caused quite a stir in New York. Her editor at *Show* had wanted her to write a puff piece, but the Playboy Club was threatening to sue and many other people were upset. Beyond being witty, Steinem's article was a serious critique of the way in which many waitresses were exploited and often not paid the wages advertised.

Steinem's article made her name well-known in New York publishing circles, but it also had unforeseen consequences for her career. Because the assignment for which she became known had not addressed a subject that was thought to be serious, she was considered a writer of "light" articles on fashion or society rather than serious political issues. She later discovered that her decision to write the Playboy article had led to the loss of many serious journalistic assignments. In later years, she came to regard the situation partly as the result of not taking her career seriously enough. She was to write:

> Though I returned an advance payment for its expansion into a book, thus avoiding drugstore racks full of paperbacks emblazoned with my name, "I Was a Playboy Bunny," and god-knows-what illustration, that article quickly became the only way I was publicly identified.... I lost a hard-won assignment to do an investigative article on the United States Information Agency, whose accurate reflection of this country I had come to doubt after seeing its operations in India.[1]

As Steinem became better known among celebrities, writers, and publishers, she began writing articles for *Glamour* magazine. Steinem was also photographed for the magazine's February, 1964 issue. Then she was selected to fly to London to interview the famous hair stylist, Vidal Sassoon. Many other interviews with famous people followed. Among them were John Lennon, the writer James Baldwin, Mary Lindsay (the wife of New York's mayor John Lindsay), the actor Michael Caine, and Dame Margot Fonteyn, the famous ballet dancer.

Her career gathered momentum, bringing her at least some of the success she had dreamed about. But she was still dissatisfied with her progress; she was not writing about the issues that most deeply concerned her. She wanted above all to write about the important political issues of the day: the fight to win civil rights for black Americans, the protests to end the war in Vietnam. Yet no matter how diligently Steinem pursued these assignments, her editors nevertheless assigned her one trivial topic after another.

In this, as in other areas, Steinem's own physical attractiveness would get in her way. It was an issue that would continue to cause her problems throughout her career. As a slender, good-looking woman, Steinem was frequently viewed by employers and the public alike with exactly the sort of stereotyping she would work hard to eliminate. Sometimes Steinem would be her own worst enemy in this—for example, by agreeing to be photographed for *Glamour*. But these incidents only showed a playful spirit that resisted categorization.

And whether they were glamorous or not, many women journalists faced the same problem: No matter how qualified they were to cover serious issues, they were usually assigned to light topics instead, usually in the fields of fashion or entertainment. Men, however, were often automatically given the serious assignments, regardless of their qualifications.

Despite these setbacks, however, Steinem never gave up. She was certain that it was only a matter of time before she would get an opportunity to tackle serious subjects. That opportunity finally came when her friend Clay Felker, an editor at *Esquire*, decided to start a new magazine. It would be called *New York* and would be designed to appeal to a sophisticated audience, with articles on contemporary culture, politics, and the arts.

From the start Felker made it clear that he wanted Steinem to be an important part of the magazine, and she didn't hesitate to commit herself. She eagerly joined in the effort to raise the substantial sums of money needed to begin the project. She became an editor, one of the people who influenced the content of the publication. She also undertook to write a weekly column. Beginning in 1968, Steinem's "The City Politic" column covered politics in New York and current sociological issues.

At the same time, she became actively involved in political causes. She took part in the 1968 presidential campaign, at first supporting Senator Eugene McCarthy in his effort to win the Democratic nomination. Then, realizing that McCarthy was not the visionary leader the nation needed, she switched her support to Senator Robert Kennedy. In a phrase that was to define many people's dissatisfaction with McCarthy, Steinem wrote in *New York* that "McCarthy thought more about McCarthy than he did about the presidency."[2]

After Robert Kennedy's tragic assassination in 1968, Steinem joined Senator George McGovern's presidential campaign. She was soon meeting with other campaign workers, planning campaign policy, outlining McGovern's stands on key issues, and gathering support.

In the midst of all this political campaigning, she also performed journalistic assignments. She was sent to cover the campaign of the Republican presidential candidate Richard Nixon. This assignment led to an interview that once again brought Steinem national attention.

Steinem had been flying on Nixon's presidential campaign plane, hoping to get an interview with the Republican candidate himself. But instead of this prize, Nixon's campaign aides delivered Patricia Nixon, the candidate's wife, who was known for her unwavering support of her husband. Typically, Pat Nixon concealed her opinions.

Initially the an interview yielded no interesting information, but then Steinem began to press Mrs. Nixon to discuss her own thoughts. Mrs. Nixon steadfastly refused. However, as the plane landed and the end of the

Pat Nixon

interview neared, Steinem struck a nerve. The candidate's wife had expressed her admiration for Mamie Eisenhower, the former first lady. Steinem responded by saying that she thought Mamie Eisenhower meant very little to young people. Somehow, this triggered a reaction in Pat Nixon. Her outburst was one of the only openly emotional moments of the Republican campaign, and revealed thoughts that were probably shared by many in Pat Nixon's generation:

> I never had time to think about things like that—who I wanted to be, or who I admired, or to have ideas. I never had time to dream about being anyone else. I had to work. My parents died when I was a teenager, and I had to work my way through college. . . . I've never had time to worry about who I admire or who I identify with. I've never had it easy. I'm not like all you . . . all those people who had it so easy.[3]

Steinem later said that she not been trying to anger Mrs. Nixon but had simply been "trying to get through to her, to show her that we had very similar childhoods. But she didn't want to know that. . . . I was just trying to make contact, and she got angry."[4]

Although Steinem's articles about current affairs were bringing her more satisfaction, she began increasingly to focus on the issues that would come to dominate her life in later years. She had not yet become identified as an articulate crusader for women's rights. But her background in politics and her serious articles during the late 1960s prepared the way.

6

The History of a Movement

Gloria Steinem's life and career changed dramatically after she attended a meeting of a New York City women's group called the Redstockings. This was in 1968, while she was gathering material for an article for *New York* magazine. The purpose of the meeting was to allow women to discuss the illegal abortions they had been forced to resort to as a result of the anti-abortion laws. Steinem had once had an illegal abortion herself, and she talked about her experience. As she listened to the other women at that meeting, she felt a growing outrage at the plight of women who were made to feel like criminals for having abortions.

The Redstockings meeting also caused Steinem to realize that many of the issues she cared about were problems shared by a large number of women. She saw clearly the double standard that kept women in inferior jobs and allowed men far more power in society. In an interview in *Newsweek* magazine in 1971, Steinem described the change:

> I'd always understood what made me angry about the Playboy Club or the double standard or not being able to do political writing or being sent out for coffee. But I didn't realize it was a group problem. Before that Redstockings meeting, I had thought that my personal problems

and experiences were my own and not part of a larger political problem.[1]

Steinem's discovery subsequently inspired her first openly feminist essay, "After Black Power, Women's Liberation." It was published in April, 1969, in *New York*, and in the article Steinem observed that many women who had fought for civil rights for blacks and against the Vietnam War were beginning to fight for political causes closer to home—specifically, equality and opportunity for women.

Steinem's article described how American women were coming to realize that theirs was a cause worth fighting for. She wrote that women were taking to the streets and demonstrating in order to make their views known on such issues as job discrimination, abortion, and child care. American women, she said, were beginning to put an end to the traditional view of women as sex objects whose main function was to please men and raise children.

Steinem made it clear that she saw the growing women's movement as unstoppable, and went on to define some of the ways in which discrimination against women in American society took place. The gap between women's and men's pay was substantial, she pointed out, and it was continually growing wider, despite the fact that the number of women in the labor force was steadily increasing.

In speaking out against the pervasive patterns of sexual discrimination in American society, Steinem was joining a long tradition of determined women who had aggressively fought to gain political equality.

What exactly was this movement that, in the late sixties, was spreading like wildfire across the United States? Simply stated, feminism was—and is—a social movement that seeks to gain equal rights and equal treatment for women. It attempts to change customs, attitudes, and laws in society so that women can have the freedom to choose their own careers and make important decisions about their own lives.

Concern for women's rights can be traced as far back as the 1700s. Before that time, the idea of equal rights for all men and women was not widely accepted. People's rights as citizens or as subjects of a monarchy were generally defined in terms of ancient traditions rather than from the perspective of democratic politics.

However, in 1792 an English writer named Mary Wollstonecraft wrote an essay "A Vindication of the Rights of Women," which was one of the first statements in English arguing for a woman's right to equality with men in education, work, and politics.

More recent, modern American influences on the feminist movement were the women suffragists who fought for the right to vote, beginning in the mid 1800s. In the United States, two women were especially important leaders in this nearly century-long battle: Elizabeth Cady Stanton and Lucretia Mott.

Stanton and Mott were active in the anti-slavery movement before they became crusaders for women's rights. In 1840 they attempted to take part in the World Anti-Slavery Convention in London, but were excluded because of their sex. Enraged by this blatant discrimination, Stanton and Mott decided to start an organization in the United States to advance the rights of women.

Eight years later, Stanton and Mott staged the Women's Rights Convention in Seneca Falls, New York. This meeting, the first organized event in the women's movement in the United States, made them famous. Three hundred people attended. The goals that were put forth there were considered revolutionary. First among them was the right to vote. "It is the duty of the women of this country," Stanton and Mott wrote, "to secure to themselves their sacred right to the elective franchise." They wrote a list of rights granted to men and demanded that the same rights be granted to women as well.

In the 1850s, the women's movement gained another forceful campaigner for the right to vote: Susan B. Anthony. In 1852 Stanton asked Anthony, who was a teacher involved in the anti-slavery movement, to help draft a petition for full property rights for women in New York. The petition called for: (1) women's control of their own earnings; (2) women's suffrage, or the right to vote; and (3) divorced women's guardianship of their children. Property rights were important because at that time it was often illegal for American women to own property after marriage. Their property automatically became the property of their husbands.

After the end of the Civil War in 1865 and the abolition of slavery, many woman abolitionists turned their attention to the fight for the right to vote. Yet in 1870, when the Fifteenth Amendment was ratified, it stated that the right to vote should not be denied because of "race, color, or previous condition of servitude." That right could still be denied because of sex.

The year 1869 saw the formation of two important women's organizations: the National Women's Suffrage

Association and the American Women's Suffrage Association. The goal of the American Women's Suffrage Association was to gain suffrage state by state rather than by a federal law. The goal of the National Women's Suffrage Association was to achieve a constitutional amendment that guaranteed suffrage nationwide. In 1875 Susan B. Anthony drew up the proposed constitutional amendment. It stated that the right of American citizens to vote should not be denied by the federal government or by the states because of a person's sex. The amendment, which would have to be passed by a two-thirds majority of both houses of Congress, was first introduced in Congress in 1878. It was not enacted.

In 1890 these two women's associations joined together to become the National American Woman Suffrage Association (NAWSA). Later, the deaths of Elizabeth Cady Stanton in 1902 and Susan B. Anthony in 1906 left the women's movement without its principal leaders. But the cause gained another forceful leader who carried on.

Alice Paul was a social worker and a feminist. She had been inspired by the courage and determination of the woman suffragists she had met in Britain, and she returned to the United States determined to energize the American women's movement. She began to teach American women political activism, using techniques she had learned from British feminists.

Paul led demonstrations and hunger strikes. She brought the issue of women's rights to the attention of the American public. In 1913, despite the opposition of a jeering crowd, she led a march of thousands of women down Pennsylvania Avenue in Washington, D.C.

Suffragettes marching for the right to vote.

At this time, however, the women's movement split over which tactics should be used in the battle for equal rights. Many women thought that women's suffrage should not become an issue of traditional party politics, but Alice Paul disagreed with this view. She organized the National Woman's Party to achieve one specific goal: the right of American women to vote. By 1916 women had obtained full suffrage in eleven states and the territory of Alaska, and partial suffrage in other states. Both major political parties had adopted women's suffrage in their political programs.

The Nineteenth Amendment, giving women the right to vote, finally passed both houses of Congress in 1919—more than forty years after it was first introduced. One year later, on August 26, 1920, it was ratified by three fourths of the states. Seventy-two years had passed since the first Women's Rights Convention at Seneca Falls.

Gaining the right to vote was a milestone in the history of American feminism. After that, the women's movement ceased to occupy as important a position in public affairs. It was not until the 1960s that women were to take their campaign for equal rights once more into the public arena.

Whereas feminists in the 1800s and early 1900s had primarily rallied around the single issue of suffrage, feminists in the 1960s began to fight for a number of other important issues. Chief among these economic and political goals was the notion of empowerment, or gaining power in order to become self-sufficient. This issue was especially important because it recalled how women's lives were controlled and limited by prejudice and discrimination.

Until the 1960s, American women were generally directed, influenced, or pressured from a very early age to consider marriage their chief goal in life. A limited number of careers was available to them, but these were generally jobs that had little status and low pay, such as teaching, nursing, and secretarial work. Often, women who were qualified for a particular job or promotion would be passed over because it was believed that only men had to support a family. Some employers also feared that women would get married or become pregnant and leave their jobs. Women were almost always paid less than men for the same type of work.

As the result of such inequality, most women were economically dependent on men. They did not have the same freedoms or opportunities to direct their own lives. Without reproductive freedom, they had little control over the size of their families. This further burdened women with the responsibilities of raising children, at a time when day care was rarely available.

Feminists thus viewed the structure of American society as inherently discriminatory against women, and they felt that as long as women had no political or economic clout, nothing would change. Thus, the feminists' fight in the 1960s entered around the need to gain political and economic power.

Although the feminist movement of the 1960s traced its origins back to the suffragists, there were more recent influences as well. One was the work of the French writer Simone de Beauvoir. Her book *The Second Sex*, published in 1953 in France, soon became a worldwide best-seller. In *The Second Sex*, de Beauvoir argued that society systematically discriminates against women to the extent that they are considered a kind of "second sex," inferior in almost every way to men. As a response, she called for the liberation of women from the widespread discrimination practiced by society. She also insisted on a point that would be taken up again and again by other feminists, including Steinem: that the liberation of women would result in the liberation of men from the stereotypes that limited their lives as well. Men would be better able to express their emotions to women if they did not see them purely as sex objects, to be impressed or used. Also, women who had been liberated from their stereotypes would be better, more interesting partners, allowing both men and women to lead fuller, more productive lives.

De Beauvoir's work outlined the patterns of thought and practice that kept women in an inferior position in society. In 1963, the American feminist Betty Friedan took up these themes in *The Feminine Mystique*, a book that profoundly influenced the feminist movement. This book gave voice to the frustrations and unvoiced ambitions of many American women. It explained how American women were tired of having their identities defined almost entirely by their roles as housewives and mothers. Friedan argued that it was time for women to step out of their confinement and seek professional satisfaction and political power instead. *The Feminine Mystique* was a huge success, not only in the United States but also throughout the world.

The climate of thought was changing rapidly, and there were other important events that altered American society. The marches and demonstrations of the civil rights struggle were absorbing the nation, and the changes in public attitudes brought about by the fight for black civil rights also helped the feminist movement.

In considering the issue of civil rights for blacks, many Americans began to realize that all prejudice was wrong, and that prejudice based on gender was as bad as prejudice based on color. The Civil Rights Act of 1964, which was primarily intended to outlaw racial discrimination, also addressed the issue of sex discrimination. It outlawed discrimination based on race, color, religion, national origin, or sex.

Yet feminists still had to fight against the views of people who believed that women were not the equals of men. In 1966 Betty Friedan and other feminists founded the National Organization for Women (NOW). Its purpose was to win an equal place for women in American society as well as American law. One of the first causes that NOW took up was the Equal Rights Amendment, or ERA. This amendment had first been introduced in Congress in 1923, through the work of the National Women's Party. It stated that "Equality of rights under the law shall not be denied or abridged by the United States or any state on account of sex."

Thus it was a movement with a rich history of political struggle and intellectual achievement that transformed Gloria Steinem's life beginning in the late 1960s. Feminists and their supporters promised to change the structure of society to allow women the same rights as men, and feminism was indeed creating a social revolution in American society. It was perhaps because Steinem herself had been no stranger to suffering, poverty, and deep disappointment that she was able to recognize and identify so readily with the issues raised by feminists. In her first openly feminist article, on the Redstockings meeting, Steinem argued for continued solidarity among women of all races and social classes. She emphasized that middle-class women should not seek to exploit the weakness and poverty of less fortunate women, but should instead work to solve their common problems.

Steinem pointed out that resistance to the women's movement would come not only from men, but from women who felt threatened by the movement's questioning of their traditional roles. This, she argued, was to be expected as a natural response from people who felt personally threatened by new ideas. Steinem emphasized, however, that the women's movement would not seek to eliminate the rights of men in order to elevate the status of women, but would make life better for both women and men. She concluded her article with this assurance: "The idea is, in the long run, that women's liberation will be men's liberation, too."[2]

7

The Feminist Emerges

So well received was Steinem's Redstockings article that a year later, in 1970, she won the Penney-Missouri Journalism Award for her reporting on the growing feminist movement. By this time, she had become well-known as a serious political journalist. But the reaction of many male colleagues to the article only reinforced her views about the difficulties faced by women who wanted to do serious work. Steinem later wrote:

> From my male friends and colleagues, however, [the article] won immediate alarm. Several took me aside kindly: Why was I writing about these crazy women instead of something serious, political, and important? How could I risk identifying myself with women's stuff when I'd worked so hard to get "real" assignments? Interestingly, the same men who had thought working as a Bunny and writing a well-publicized article was just fine for my career were now cautionary about one brief article on a political movement among women.[1]

Gloria Steinem had always resisted outside pressures, and now she used these comments to examine how she herself had been affected by society's stereotyping of women. She concluded that the worst aspect of sex discrimination is that it causes women to doubt their own abilities.

> That was the worst of it, of course—my own capitulation to all the small humiliations, and my own refusal to trust an emotional understanding of what was going on, or even to trust my own experience. For instance, I had believed that women couldn't get along with one another, even while my own most trusted friends were women. I had agreed that women were more "conservative" even while I identified emotionally with every discriminated-against group. . . . It is truly amazing how long we can go on accepting myths that oppose our own lives, assuming instead that we are the odd exceptions.[2]

Steinem's efforts to write more about women's issues were greeted with skepticism or downright hostility by many editors. Most news magazines insisted that there was little need for articles about feminism. Some editors, Steinem said, actually argued that if a magazine were to publish one article that advocated equality for women, it would then have to publish another article arguing against equality, simply to prove that it was "objective" about the issue. Frustrated, Steinem turned to the lecture circuit instead of writing, "in order to report the deeper realities" that she had first glimpsed the night of that abortion meeting. "That was the beginning," she wrote. "But not the end. The first flash of consciousness reveals so much that it seems like the sun coming up. In fact, it's more like a first candle in the dark."[3]

Whether a rising sun or a candle in the dark, Steinem's new consciousness of feminism was a light that began to illuminate her life. It showed her that the issues of women's rights affected not just herself but the lives of all women.

Steinem also began to find that the issues were connected in many more ways than she had ever expected. She discovered, for example, that for women, the most important political issues concerned domestic problems, such as child care and housework. Most male politicians, however, continued to insist that domestic issues were less important than the so-called "larger issues" such as foreign affairs or the military budget.

One of the most obvious areas of public life in which women could work to gain greater influence, and bring these issues to the fore, was in state and federal government. During the early 1970s, few women held government offices. But women's groups soon started to focus on electing women to Congress and state legislatures.

The National Women's Political Caucus was founded to further women's political participation. Organized in 1971, the NWPC was the brainchild of Steinem, Betty Friedan, and two congresswomen from New York, Bella Abzug and Shirley Chisholm. Abzug and Chisholm supported feminist issues and, as prominent women, served as important role models for many ambitious young women interested in entering politics.

Gradually, Steinem found that more and more of her time was being devoted to tasks not directly related to her writing. Organizing events for feminist causes was very time-consuming, but she was often asked to do it because she was so good at it. This meant that she had

Betty Friedan

less time to devote to her writing. In fact, most of her writing during this period was devoted to furthering the political movements she supported. For example, Steinem wrote the guiding principles for the National Women's Political Caucus. Yet all the activities of her life soon came together in a new enterprise that was to be her central concern for the next decade.

Steinem and others realized that feminism, while not yet a household word, was gaining a national following. Conquering her fears about facing large audiences, she began to speak out in public appearances across the nation, defining the goals of feminism and asking for support. The response at such events was overwhelming.

Thousands of women and men who came to hear Steinem expressed their support for women's issues. In addition, more and more women joined Steinem in speaking out. Steinem saw that the women's movement could grow into a fundamental social revolution, and this vision called for even more effective ways to reach out to greater numbers of American women.

Steinem realized that many women outside major metropolitan areas did not have the support they needed to speak out about their problems. In response to this need, she founded the Women's Action Alliance, whose purpose was to develop educational programs and services to assist women and women's organizations.

Women who worked for the Alliance thought that a newsletter or magazine providing information relevant to the concerns of women could help, and Steinem soon became very interested in the project. She began holding meetings in her apartment to discuss it.

The women involved in those early discussions would become nationally important figures in the feminist movement: Jane O'Reilly, Cathy O'Hair, Letty Cottin Pogrebin, Joanne Edgar, Mary Peacock, and Florynce Kennedy, among others. These women eventually decided to create a magazine specifically for women and women's issues. After much discussion, they decided that the title of the magazine would be *Ms.* ("Ms." is a non-sexist term created by feminists to refer to a woman without designating her marital status, as the terms Mrs. and Miss do.)

Steinem and the others were willing to do all the work necessary to start the magazine. But taking on such a momentous project requires more than just hard work.

It requires huge sums of money, to set up an office and pay the salaries of the people who will produce the magazine.

Steinem and her colleagues began fund-raising for their project. However, most potential investors felt unsure that *Ms.* would succeed and were therefore unwilling to risk large amounts of money. The prospects for starting up the nation's first feminist magazine looked bleak.

Fortunately, Clay Felker, Steinem's friend and colleague from *New York* magazine, had a helpful proposition. He suggested that Steinem create a first issue of the magazine and publish it as a supplement to a regular December issue of *New York*. If Steinem and her colleagues would do all the editorial work, he would provide the printing and production without charge. The offer was generous, and Steinem accepted it. All the women involved agreed that it was an excellent chance to try out the new magazine.

On December 20, 1971, *New York* magazine came out with the test issue of *Ms.* The new magazine was an immediate success. In fact, it met with so much approval that the the supplement was quickly expanded to a preview issue of *Ms.*, which came out in January, 1972.

The day that first issue of *Ms.* came out, Steinem was in California doing publicity for the magazine. She learned that people were having difficulty finding copies of *Ms.* at newsstands there. Worried that something had interrupted distribution of the new issue, she telephoned the delivery centers, only to learn that the magazine had already been distributed. People were having difficulty finding *Ms.* because in most places it was sold out.

Ms. helped many women discuss for the first time feminism and its effect on their lives. In 1972, the magazine's first year, Steinem wrote an article for *Ms.* entitled "Sisterhood," about the sense of solidarity that she felt with all women, regardless of race, class, or politics:

> At first my discoveries seemed personal. In fact, they were the same ones so many millions of women have made and are continuing to make. Greatly simplified, they go like this: Women are human beings first, with minor differences from men that apply largely to the single act of reproduction. We share the dreams, capabilities, and weaknesses of all human beings, but our occasional pregnancies and other visible differences have been used—even more pervasively, if less brutally, than racial differences have been used—to create an "inferior" group and an elaborate division of labor. The division is continued for a clear if often unconscious reason: the economic and social profit of males as a group.
>
> Once this feminist realization dawned, I reacted in what turned out to be predictable ways. First, I was amazed at the simplicity and obviousness of a realization that made sense, at last, of my life experience. I couldn't figure out why I hadn't seen it before. Second, I realized how far that new vision of life was from the system around us, and how tough it would be to explain this feminist realization at all, much less to get people (especially, though not only, men) to accept so drastic a change.[4]

Steinem described in this article how she came to develop a sense of self through feminism. This discovery, she wrote, changed her perspective, her life, and her relationships with men and women. In choosing the title "Sisterhood," she emphasized that women would need to be sisters to one another in order to withstand the pressures and prejudices of a system that had not granted them equality.

Yet even while insisting that women would have to fight to achieve equal status, Steinem asserted that the women's movement was good news for both women and men. Time and time again she emphasized that feminism would be as rewarding for men as for women. This was because feminism would liberate men from stereotypes that limited their own behavior and opportunities as much as they limited those of women.

It was no accident that Steinem's feminism eventually led her to create *Ms.* magazine. She had considered herself a writer for almost as long as she could remember. *Ms.* gave her a way to employ her writing talents in support of a cause that gave new meaning to her life. Steinem concluded "Sisterhood" with these words:

I finally understand why for years I have identified with "out" groups: I belong to one, too. And I know it will take a coalition of such groups to achieve a society in which, at a minimum, no one is born into a second-class role because of visible difference, because of race or of sex.[5]

Steinem at the Democratic National Convention, 1972.

8

Woman of the Year

The year 1972 was an election year, and the campaigning promised to be intense. Gloria Steinem, as usual, did not hesitate to enter the fray. The Democratic National Convention that year offered a particularly important opportunity to fight for a central feminist issue: reproductive freedom, or a woman's right to make her own decisions about birth control and abortion.

Feminists had long considered reproductive freedom one of a woman's most important rights. The National Women's Political Caucus, for which Steinem had been working, decided that the 1972 Democratic Convention would be an ideal opportunity for feminists to try to place reproductive freedom on the political agenda. Specifically, the NWPC wanted to include a guarantee of reproductive freedom in the Democratic party platform.

Steinem had enjoyed a long friendship with Senator George McGovern of South Dakota, one of the front-runners for the Democratic nomination. She had worked for his campaign in 1968. In 1972, she used her influence to set up a meeting between McGovern and the NWPC to discuss the inclusion of a reproductive freedom plank in the party's platform for the coming election. McGovern was sympathetic to the views of Steinem and her colleagues. However, in an attempt to satisfy supporters of a variety of causes, he eventually allowed the statement about reproductive freedom to be kept out of the party's platform.

Steinem did not give up. Insisting that women's issues should be discussed at the convention, she went there as a representative of the National Women's Political Caucus. But instead of supporting McGovern for the nomination, Steinem supported Shirley Chisholm, the black congresswoman from New York. The reason she gave for her switch was that women should do everything they could to support a woman candidate. Chisholm's candidacy was deserving, said Steinem, if only because it suggested that a woman could be elected president.

The 1972 convention was a thrilling event for all those promoting women's issues there. Political conventions always involve battles for power between different political factions. This one was no different. A women's caucus, or interest group, however, ensured that women representatives would be organized and ready for issue-oriented floor fights. Caucus members had prepared a list of objectives they wanted to include in the party platform. They fought to make their views heard and to see that women held positions of leadership in state delegations.

At the end of the convention, Steinem and her colleagues looked back with satisfaction on the achievements of the women's caucus. They had succeeded in getting most of their objectives written into the party platform—with the exception of the right to reproductive freedom. And thanks to their efforts, the participation of women in the convention hit an all-time high. Before 1972, there had been almost no mention of women's issues in the platforms of the established political parties. At least now one party had taken a step in the right direction.

Steinem later stated that "women are never again going to be mindless coffee-makers or mindless policy-makers in politics. . . . We have to learn to lead ourselves."[1] Unquestionably, she was learning to lead. She had become a well-known public speaker, an active participant in Democratic party politics, a founding member of several important women's organizations, and one of the founding editors of a national magazine.

Since she was now a celebrity herself, Steinem had to turn down requests for interviews. News magazines, however, insisted on publishing articles about the woman who was such a visible spokesperson for the growing feminist movement. In the several years following her political emergence in 1970, Steinem appeared on no fewer than ten network television shows, wrote an article on the women's movement for *Time* magazine, and appeared on the cover of *Newsweek*. In addition, she was the subject of innumerable newspaper articles throughout the country.

In 1972, Gloria Steinem was chosen "Woman of the Year" by *McCall's* magazine. Citing her many accomplishments, the magazine wrote that Steinem had become the most effective symbol of and spokesperson for the women's movement: "Gloria Steinem has become a household word at a time in history when the American household is the scene of action in a widespread cultural revolution."[2]

McCall's went on to describe how ordinary Americans reacted to Steinem on her frequent lecture tours across the country. The magazine wrote that even in the generally conservative area of Wichita, Kansas, Steinem drew great sympathy from the huge crowds of people who came to hear her speak: "An astonishingly wide spectrum of women—factory workers and Junior Leaguers, student radicals and Establishment conservatives—respond to her."[3]

Steinem, however, did not regard her new fame with uncritical enthusiasm. She consented only reluctantly to interviews, which took valuable time away from other important activities. And as with all celebrities who occupy a prominent position in public life, the interviews and articles were sometimes far from complimentary.

One article that appeared in *Esquire* magazine in 1971 was especially disturbing to her. Entitled "She: The Awesome Power of Gloria Steinem," the article presented a scathing view of Steinem's success. *Esquire*'s readership was mainly male, the type of audience most likely to be threatened by the ideas and political views that Steinem represented. The article described her rise as primarily the result of her beauty and her skill in manipulating rich and famous people.

Steinem was very upset with what the article implied about her career. She even thought of suing the magazine, but decided against it. Steinem later realized that the *Esquire* article was an example of the type of unjustified criticism suffered by many women who achieve public prominence in their careers. As she later told *McCall's*, "I don't mind people attacking me on issues . . . but I mind sexist attack."[4]

But even some feminists were critical of Steinem and her colleagues at *Ms.* especially about the role of the magazine. In fact, *Ms.* itself was often a center of controversy within the feminist movement. Revolutionary movements always bring together people who share the same goals but hold different views about the tactics to be used in achieving them. Those who are more radical often come into conflict with others who are less extreme.

Therefore, it was not surprising when some radical feminists began accusing Steinem and her associates at *Ms.* of having betrayed the feminist movement. They argued that *Ms.* was not radical enough. They claimed that the magazine sought to accommodate men, rather than confront them, when it attacked sex discrimination or addressed feminist issues.

Some radical feminists rejected *Ms.*'s battle for equal rights altogether. Many of these were Marxists—followers of the ideas and political theories of the German philosopher Karl Marx, who argued that different classes were continually battling one another and that true justice would result only from the overthrow of capitalism. Some radical Marxist feminists argued that achieving equal rights in American society was impossible. American society, they claimed, was too devoted to its capitalist way of life for real equality to ever take hold. What was needed, they insisted, was a revolution that would completely change the capitalist system in the United States.

Steinem and the other *Ms.* editors defended their position and argued that there were many ways to work for feminist goals, and theirs was the best way they knew how. One radical feminist, Vivian Gornick, entered the debate and wrote admiringly of the achievements of Steinem and her colleagues:

A number of years ago, about fifty women gathered in Gloria Steinem's living room to discuss the possibility of starting a feminist magazine. The women in that room occupied every space on the feminist political spectrum I'd ever heard of, and some I'd never heard of. Everyone had different ideas and different approaches to the question of a feminist magazine. . . . The exchange went on for hours. Meanwhile, at one end of the room sat a number of well-dressed women quietly jotting figures on paper: women who clearly knew how capitalist enterprise works. The upshot was, I (and everyone else like me) walked away from that meeting, went back to my working life, and forgot about the magazine. Gloria Steinem and her friends with the pieces of paper went seriously at it, and the result was *Ms.*[5]

Despite or perhaps because of the controversies that occasionally befell her at *Ms.*, Steinem continued to pursue the work she considered important. She came to devote more and more time to the projects she believed were beneficial to American women. Typical of such projects was one she helped to establish with *Ms.*—the Ms. Foundation for Women. This organization granted money for the establishment of women's groups and for projects committed to helping women in their local communities.

Steinem was also active in forming the Coalition of Labor Union Women, a group that helped women who wanted to create new labor unions or gain better representation in existing ones. In Steinem's opinion, the Coalition of Labor Union Women could be particularly effective fighting against sexual discrimination in the workplace.

The early 1970s was an extremely busy time for Steinem. In 1974, she celebrated her fortieth birthday. The occasion offerred a chance for her to reflect on her life and career, to look back at the events of past from the perspective of her recent successes. Asked how she felt about turning forty, she insisted that, rather than feeling worried about growing old, she was looking forward to new accomplishments in the future. When someone remarked that she didn't look forty years old, she responded with a comment that became famous among

With Democratic presidential candidate Edmund Muskie.

feminists: "This is what forty looks like. We've been lying for so long, who would know?"[6]

One year later, in 1975, Steinem's personal life changed dramatically when she met Stan Pottinger, the man with whom she would be involved for many years. Pottinger was a lawyer who worked in the Civil Rights Division of the Justice Department in Washington, D.C. Steinem met him in New York at a meeting where he had been assigned to discuss sex discrimination cases.

Pottinger shared Steinem's interest in women's issues, actively supporting her work for passage of the ERA. He had been married and divorced and was raising two small children, so he was well acquainted with the problems faced by women who had to raise families by themselves.

Steinem and Pottinger found themselves meeting frequently, either in New York or in Washington. But Steinem was now so busy that time became a problem. On Friday afternoons she frequently found herself rushing from her office at *Ms.* to the airport, so she could fly down to Washington and spend the weekends with Pottinger. Her new relationship, though, brought her happiness and led to an unexpected harmony between her personal and professional lives.

9

The Battle for the ERA

Gloria Steinem's work took on an international cast in 1975. This would be International Women's Year, declared by the United Nations. By designating the year as one devoted to women, the U.N. hoped to call the world's attention to important issues that affected women everywhere. In industrialized nations, these issues concerned equal rights and equal economic opportunities. In the poorer non-industrialized countries, however, women faced more basic problems: hunger, nutrition, adequate shelter, birth control.

The highlight of International Women's Year was a week-long conference in Mexico City in June, 1975. Delegates from nations throughout the world gathered there to discuss the problems of women in their countries. Steinem travelled to the conference as a journalist and had been invited to speak before a group of reporters from developing nations at a meeting that preceded the conference.

The conference included discussions, speeches, and workshops on topics ranging from the care of babies to the role of women in politics and the work force. In general, however, it was a disappointment for Steinem and other feminists. They had hoped the conference would be a means of bringing together women from different nations and cultures. Instead, it sparked confrontation between groups with different political views.

Some delegates had been instructed by their governments to pursue political objectives rather than specific women's issues. One example was a resolution that condemned Zionism as racism. Zionism is the movement of the Jewish people to establish and maintain Judaism and the nation of Israel. At the conference, Palestinian participants and their supporters insisted on this resolution. Most American feminists, however, considered the resolution a conflict that distracted delegates from more important feminist issues.

Steinem returned to the United States disillusioned. She was outraged that governments, run primarily by men, had used the women's movement to create conflict between women's groups.

She could not dwell on her disillusionment long, however. A pressing issue closer to home demanded her attention: the Equal Rights Amendment. The essential principle of the ERA was that sex should have no place in determining people's legal rights. Introduced in Congress for the first time in 1923, Congress finally passed the ERA in 1972, under pressure from Steinem and other feminists. This was only the beginning, however. The amendment would have to be ratified, or accepted, by three-fourths of the state legislatures. And for that to happen, the general public would have to be persuaded to accept the amendment.

Within one year of its approval by Congress, the ERA was ratified by thirty states. But opposition also began to mount. Conservative religious and political organizations led a campaign against the amendment. One of the chief groups fighting against the ERA was led by a woman—Phyllis Schlafly.

Schlafly's Stop-ERA organization based its opposition to the ERA on fears that women would lose special privileges and protections if the amendment passed. They claimed, for example, that the ERA would force women to perform active combat duty in the military, and that, under the ERA, divorced women with children would no longer receive economic support from their husbands.

In response, supporters of the ERA argued that a constitutional amendment was necessary because laws in some states and even some federal laws were biased against women. The National Organization for Women was the chief organization supporting the ERA. NOW members, including Steinem, conducted a broad campaign to educate Americans about the benefits of the amendment. They insisted that hundreds of laws discriminated against women and kept them in a state of economic dependence on men.

Steinem took an active role in the fight to ratify the ERA. She wrote articles about the advantages of the amendment. She raised the issue in interviews with prominent people. She argued for the amendment in debates and lectures. She even crusaded for the ERA as host of a public television series, supported by *Ms.*, called "Women Alive".

The battle to pass the ERA took up much of Steinem's time and energy, even as she continued with her responsibilities at *Ms.* Then, in 1977, she began yet another nationwide project. Two years earlier, congresswomen Bella Abzug and Patsy Mink had proposed that a public conference be held in every state to discuss issues concerning women and elect delegates to a national women's conference. The purpose of the national conference would be to study women's issues and then recommend ways that specific laws could be changed to remove barriers to women's equality.

President Jimmy Carter supported the project and authorized a group of about forty women, including Steinem, to establish an International Women's Year - commission. The commission held two-day conferences in every state to elect delegates to a national women's conference, which was planned for Houston that November. Both the initial two-day meetings and the national conference were huge successes.

Steinem later described the events as the result of months of work by women throughout the nation. Each two-day conference was attended by as many as twenty thousand women and men. Calling the conferences the largest and most representative statewide political meetings ever held for feminist issues, Steinem praised the fact that they had identified many of the most important obstacles to equality for women in the United States.

At the four-day conference, participants debated and voted on recommendations developed at the state meetings. Because of the broad level of support that had evolved, the resolutions passed by the delegates earned the support of a majority of Americans, women and men.

For Steinem, one of the most heartening aspects of the conference was that it allowed many groups of women previously unheard in public affairs to voice their grievances openly. They included homemakers, widows of coal miners, black women of all social classes, blue-collar women, and many other hard-working but little-known Americans.

Steinem was especially honored to be appointed the scribe, or official recorder, for several minority women's groups. She described the two sleepless days in which she worked in that capacity as one of the high points of her life. She felt a sense of triumph when she realized that women could bridge the barriers of race that had so often separated them in the past. She noted with pride that more than a third of the delegates at the conference were women of color, and that these included not only black but Latina, Asian American, Alaskan, and Native American women. Gloria Steinem later described her sense of victory:

> For myself, Houston and all the events surrounding it have become a landmark in personal history, the sort of milestone that divides our sense of time. Figuring out the date of any other event now means remembering: Was it before or after Houston? . . . I had learned, finally, that *individual women* could be competent, courageous, and loyal to each other. Despite growing up with no experience of women in positions of worldly authority, I had learned that much. But I still did not believe that *women as a group* could be competent, courageous, and loyal to each other. I didn't believe that we could conduct large, complex events that celebrated our own diversity. I wasn't sure that we could make a history that was our own.
>
> But we can. Houston taught us that. The question is: Will this lesson be lost again?[1]

Much of Steinem's work during the next years would be devoted to ensuring that the lessons of Houston would not be lost. Shortly after returning to New York from the conference, she received a Woodrow Wilson Fellowship from the Smithsonian Institution. It would allow her to live in Washington for a year to study how feminism affects society and politics in the United States.

Steinem needed the time in Washington to concentrate on her writing. She had been so busy organizing and raising funds that she hadn't had as much time to write as she had hoped. She was also looking forward to spending more time with her family. Her sister Susanne still lived in Washington, as did her mother. Ruth had been in a hospital for a time but was now living on her own in an apartment. Her health was failing, and Steinem was glad to be able to care for her again.

10

Triumphs and Tragedies

While in Washington, Steinem studied feminist theories. True to her style, however, she didn't lose touch with the current struggles themselves. One issue that kept her busy throughout 1978 was the status of the ERA.

By this time, the amendment was close to becoming law. Only three more states were needed to ratify the amendment—but those three states were becoming extremely difficult to find. Opposition to the ERA was increasing at an alarming rate. Virginia, an important state, did not pass the amendment. And the deadline established for passage of the ERA was fast approaching—March, 1979.

The vote in the Illinois state legislature was an important test for feminists. Supporters of the ERA worked hard to persuade legislators to approve it. However, in June, 1978, the ERA was defeated. The amendment went to a second vote in Illinois several weeks later, but again it was defeated. Supporters of the ERA were deeply frustrated. Their hopes for meeting the 1979 deadline were dim.

Steinem was very much involved in the struggle for the ERA. She and other feminists used every means at their disposal to support its passage. Some feminists organized boycotts in states that had not passed the ERA—women were encouraged to refuse to buy products from, travel to, or do business in such states.

The National Organization for Women decided to organize a large march on Washington to publicize the plight of the ERA and to pressure Congress to extend the deadline for its ratification. The Women's March on Washington, often called the ERA Extension March, was reminiscent of the famous March on Washington by civil rights groups in 1963. That march had been the occasion of Martin Luther King's epic "I Have a Dream" speech. Feminists hoped that the women's march would attract huge numbers of people, which would in turn create such an impressive show of votes that lawmakers would be persuaded to extend the ERA deadline.

The march was set for July 9, 1978—the anniversary of the death of the respected suffragist and feminist Alice Paul. The march itself was designed to recreate an earlier women's march that had been held to demand the right to vote. The marchers wore white and carried banners colored in purple, gold, and white in honor of the early suffragists. They even walked along the same route that the suffragists had taken. They also commemorated a spot where men opposed to the suffragists had attacked and beaten them.

The organizers of the march had hoped for a crowd of about twenty-five thousand supporters and spectators. But the day of the march was very hot and humid, and many feared the weather might keep people away. At eleven in the morning, however, as the march began, busloads of supporters began arriving at the site.

The march was a greater success than even its most optimistic organizers had hoped. Newspaper estimates placed the crowd at about one hundred thousand people. That made the march the largest gathering for the cause

The Women's March on Washington: July 9, 1978.

of women's rights in history. The march had indeed been a show of political might—and Congress appeared to take note. Whether from sympathy for the ERA or out of respect for the large number of voters who supported it, Congress finally granted an extension for its passage. The new deadline was to be June 30, 1982.

Despite the success of the ERA Extension March, however, Steinem understood that there was much hard work to be done if the ERA was ever to become law. She did not underestimate the difficulties in the fight for ratification.

One of the most important and difficult tasks was to educate the public about the true meaning of the ERA. Steinem wrote that the news media, which could have been helpful in educating the public, was doing relatively little. She also described her anger and frustration at the false claims that many anti-ERA groups were making about the effects the amendment would have. The ERA would not lead to the abolishment of separate bathrooms for men and women, or to a female military draft. Steinem wrote:

> The Equal Rights Amendment began its long ratification process in 1972, yet to my knowledge, not one major newspaper or radio station, not one network news department or national television show, has ever done an independent investigative report on what the ERA will and will not do.
>
> Instead, the major media have been content to present occasional interviews, debates, and contradictory reports from those who are for or

against. One expert is quoted as saying that the ERA will strengthen the legal rights of women in general and homemakers in particular by causing the courts to view marriage as a partnership, and the next one says the ERA will force wives to work outside the home and eliminate alimony. One political leader explains on camera that the ERA protects women and men from discriminatory federal laws; then another politician calls the ERA a federal power grab that will reduce individual rights. One activist says that the ERA is a simple guarantee of democracy that should have been part of the Bill of Rights, had the Constitution not been written by and for property-owning white males, and the next one insists it will destroy the family, eliminate heterosexuality, and integrate bathrooms.

Understandably, the audience is confused. [But] reading or hearing the actual twenty-four words of the ERA is the most reliable path to its support. Many people are still surprised to learn that there's no mention of *unisex* or *abortion* or combat in its text; such is the confusion created by anti-ERA arguments. Yet most ERA news coverage never quotes its text at all.[1]

In Washington Steinem was occupied not only with her work in support of the ERA but also with research for her Woodrow Wilson Fellowship. In addition, she kept up her work for *Ms.*, writing several articles for the magazine and keeping in touch with her colleagues there. Often she returned to New York on weekends.

Steinem also continued to lecture and participate in fund-raising events. One speech was of special significance—the commencement address at the Antioch School of Law in Washington. Steinem's sister, Susanne Patch, was a member of the graduating class of 1978—she had raised a family and then gone back to school to earn a law degree. Steinem was very proud of her sister. She saw that despite the different choices she and Susanne had made in life, Susanne had retained the energy and independence that Steinem herself often felt they had both inherited from their mother.

Susanne's graduation turned out to be one of the last family triumphs that Ruth Steinem would live to see. She died in 1981. For Gloria and Susanne, it was a painful loss. They had both experienced all the difficulties and traumas of their mother's troubled life. During the last decade, however, they had also watched her win many battles in her unending fight against her illness. So much had changed, in fact, that now it was easier for Steinem to recall the moments of triumph and happiness in her mother's life than to remember all the tragedies and all the fears.

After the funeral, she took stock of her mother's possessions. Among them, she found a manuscript of a journal that Ruth Steinem had kept during a recent trip to Europe. The discovery of this journal, which she had never known about, showed her that her mother had continued writing even late in her life.

Steinem later published a tribute to the memory of her mother entitled "Ruth's Song (Because She Could Not Sing It)." She described movingly how her mother had been forced to suppress her own ambitions and values, eventually giving up her career entirely, in order to raise a family with a financially irresponsible husband. She also revealed the tremendous pressure she herself had felt when, as a child, she had been required to care for a mentally disturbed parent:

> She was a loving, intelligent, terrorized woman who tried hard to clean our littered house whenever she emerged from her private world, but who could rarely be counted on to finish one task. In many ways, our roles were reversed: I was the mother and she was the child. Yet that didn't help her, for she still worried about me with all the intensity of a frightened mother, plus the special fears of her own world full of threats and hostile voices.
>
> Even then I suppose I must have known that, years before she was thirty-five and I was born, she had been a spirited, adventurous young woman who struggled out of a working-class family and into college, who found work she loved and continued to do, even after she was married and my older sister was there to be cared for. Certainly, our immediate family and nearby relatives, of whom I was by far the youngest, must have remembered her life as a whole and functioning person. She was thirty before she gave up her own career to help my father run the Michigan summer resort that was the most practical of his many dreams, and she worked hard there as everything from bookkeeper to bar manager. The family must have watched this

energetic, fun-loving, book-loving woman turn into someone who was afraid to be alone, who could not hang on to reality long enough to hold a job, and who could rarely concentrate enough to read a book.[2]

At this point in her life, Steinem was able to understand the experience of her mother's life from the perspective gained from years of work in the women's movement. She was convinced that feminism had changed the lives of many women for the better. She also couldn't help feeling that her mother's life, too, could have been changed if she had been able to benefit from the achievements of the women's movement. Steinem concluded :

> I miss her, but perhaps no more in death than I did in life. Dying seems less sad than having lived too little. But at least we're now asking questions about all the Ruths and all our family mysteries.
>
> If her song inspires that, I think she would be the first to say: It was worth the singing.[3]

11

The Future of Feminism

As the June 30, 1982, deadline approached, it seemed less and less likely that the ERA would be ratified. The approval of only three more states—out of fifteen that had not yet ratified the amendment—was necessary, but opposition in those states was strong. Polls showed that a majority of Americans supported the ideals represented by the ERA, but passive agreement was much different from active support. The election in 1980 of Ronald Reagan, the conservative Republican president, meant that the ERA—and feminist goals in general—faced hostile opposition from the federal government. By late spring of 1982, many ERA supporters were already conceding defeat.

In June, just weeks before the final deadline of the ERA, the staff of *Ms.* prepared for a bittersweet celebration: the tenth anniversary of the founding of the magazine. More than a thousand people were invited to a party in New York.

There was food, drink, music, and dancing. The guests enjoyed themselves as best they could. Pat Carbine, the publisher of *Ms.*, insisted that the women's movement would rebound from this temporary defeat. Steinem spoke about the tremendous changes that the women's movement had created in American society during the past decade. She pointed out that almost every American city and town now had a women's center or a counseling service, where very few had existed before.

Steinem at an ERA rally in 1981.

However, there was no mistaking the fact that many people were angry and disappointed.

Still, the disappointment over the ERA's failure did not deter Steinem from continuing with her work. Many of her friends had been encouraging her for years to publish a book. Letty Cottin Pogrebin, Steinem's colleague at Ms., had shown some of her essays to a publisher, who expressed great interest in publishing a collection.

Soon Steinem began the difficult task of reading through the many essays, articles, and speeches she had prepared over the past twenty years. Each article had to be reread, edited, and updated. In 1983, the book, *Outrageous Acts and Everyday Rebellions,* was published. Critical praise followed swiftly. A reviewer for the *New York Times Book Review* praised the "intelligence, restraint and common sense" of the work and wrote admiringly of "the energetic and involved life" it reflected.[1]

Outrageous Acts included well-known and lesser known articles from Steinem's publications, articles that inspired great admiration and essays that shocked people as much in the 1980s as they had when they were first published. Two essays were completely new. One was the introduction, in which Steinem reflected on the meaning of her long career as a journalist and her two decades of involvement with feminist issues. This introductory essay described the difficulties that she and other women writers had faced early in their careers, when male editors and publishers routinely refused to take women and women's issues seriously.

The other new essay was "Ruth's Song," which struck a sympathetic chord in many women and men who had family members who had suffered from mental illness. Steinem received many letters of thanks from such people, who told her that she had made it easier for them to understand and speak about their similar experiences.

Her book provoked curiosity and even outrage from some people who did not understand what she meant by the title, which appeared to encourage social rebellion through "outrageous acts." When reporters asked Steinem to explain this term, she responded that she wanted women to change their lives by starting with small things. By committing at least one outrageous act per day, she said, women could gradually change society's attitudes about what women could and could not do.

Such acts might be as simple as a housewife's refusal to clean up after her husband, or as ambitious as a woman labor leader's attempt to organize a strike to protest working conditions. If women continued to perform such acts day after day, Steinem said, one day the world would be a very different, and much better, place.

Steinem enjoyed the publicity tours that followed the publication of the book. She traveled to England and Japan and discovered once again that women faced greater obstacles to social inequality in other countries, particularly in Japan, than they did in the United States.

Publicity events also included media interviews. One time Steinem appeared as a featured guest on the television interview show "20/20," hosted by Barbara Walters. In response to Walters' request and to the delight of the audience, Steinem called upon the talents of her childhood and tap-danced to a song sung by Walters herself.

With Jane Fonda and Carole King on "The Merv Griffin Show."

Steinem's sense of humor and her ability to take herself lightly brought her great popularity and close friendships, but it occasionally had negative effects. For a feature article in the November 1, 1983, *People* magazine, she agreed to pose for a photograph that showed her relaxing in a bathtub. Steinem's body was completely hidden behind a huge pile of soap bubbles, with only her smiling face visible above the top. The photograph inspired both laughter and outrage.

Most people found it funny, but others felt it was inappropriate for a feminist leader to place herself in what they saw as a demeaning pose. Steinem agreed that she should not have posed for the photograph.

March, 1984, marked Steinem's fiftieth birthday. Her friends and colleagues threw a huge party that celebrated the occasion in fitting style. More than seven hundred guests were invited to the grand ballroom of the Waldorf

Astoria Hotel—media celebrities, publishing executives, leaders of the women's movement, writers, journalists, editors, and many other people who had known Steinem in her long career. An all-woman band played music for the occasion, and Steinem was honored with a song composed in her honor.

Among the famous guests at the birthday party were Rosa Parks, the woman who began the civil rights movement by refusing to give up her seat to a white rider on a segregated bus, and Sally Ride, the first American female astronaut. *Newsweek* magazine wrote that "At 50, Steinem remains prominently and totally involved in a social revolution that is entering its third decade."[2] *Newsweek* quoted the British feminist Germaine Greer as saying that the success of Steinem's recent book proved that she had great support among women, and that "there are hundreds and thousands of women out there who still look to her."[3]

It may have been the success of Steinem's *Outrageous Acts* that encouraged her to complete yet another book project. This was a biography of a woman who at first seemed an unlikely subject for a feminist writer: the sex symbol and movie star Marilyn Monroe. Monroe had died tragically in 1963 at the age of 36 from an overdose of sleeping pills. She had starred in several well-known films made during the 1950s, including *Gentlemen Prefer Blondes, How to Marry a Millionaire, Bus Stop,* and *Some Like It Hot.* Monroe had widely publicized marriages to the baseball star Joe DiMaggio and the playwright Arthur Miller. Her public image had been that of a sensitive, deeply insecure woman who was destroyed by the pressures of Hollywood.

The book, which was published in 1986, presented a sympathetic view of Monroe and her conflicts with the male-dominated world of the film industry. Steinem saw in the patterns of Monroe's life many dilemmas common to the lives of all American women, who confront pressures from a society that constantly makes them feel insecure and afraid. The lessons of Monroe's life and death, Steinem said, highlighted the fact that women could benefit far more by acting together than by acting alone.

Steinem's biography of Monroe was both a popular and critical success. One reviewer in the *New York Times* wrote that *Marilyn* was a "well-researched book" with "none of the sensationalism that has colored other purportedly serious books about the film star."[4]

Even as Steinem's books gained great success, however, *Ms.* magazine began to encounter difficulties. For many years, *Ms.* had remained the premier monthly publication addressing serious women's issues. However, by the mid-1980s, many other magazines had begun publishing the sort of articles on women's issues that *Ms.* had pioneered. The growing competition from other magazines led to a decline in readership, and so advertising revenues also declined.

In 1987, *Ms.* was was sold to an Australian media firm, John Fairfax, Ltd., for a price that was rumored to be about $15 million. Despite Fairfax's infusion of cash, however, *Ms.* continued to have difficulties. In November 1989, after sixteen years in business, the owners of *Ms.* allowed the magazine to go into bankruptcy. Steinem was deeply disappointed.

Hope remained, however, that *Ms.* could be revived

in an altered format. Steinem, who never let misfortune get the better of her, began working toward this possibility. By the spring of 1990, plans had been established to create a new *Ms.* magazine. This time, it would take the form of a reader-supported journal.

The new magazine would have no advertising, so it would be much more independent than the old *Ms.*, which had often been forced to moderate its feminist views in order to avoid offending corporate advertisers. The new *Ms.* would publish serious articles on contemporary feminist issues, as well as poetry, fiction, and political cartoons. It would also republish some old articles that had become famous examples of feminist literature. The chief editor of *Ms.* was to be the prominent feminist leader and author, Robin Morgan. Gloria Steinem would be a consulting editor and frequent contributor to the magazine. The first issue of the new *Ms.* appeared on the newsstands in July, 1990. Thus, Steinem's long-held vision of a national magazine by, for, and about women remained alive.

At the beginning of the 1990s, Steinem could look back with satisfaction on three decades of work in journalism and the feminist movement. Despite many frustrations and failures, and despite ongoing sexual discrimination, she had succeeded in becoming the professional writer she had dreamed of being since childhood. The girl from Toledo, Ohio, who had cared for her sick mother through times of bitter poverty, had become a prize-winning journalist, the leader of a social revolution, and the symbol of a new era for women in America.

And what of the feminist movement itself, for which Steinem had worked so hard and endured so much? After the activism of the 1960s and 1970s, the mood of the nation in the 1980s seemed to change sharply. Fewer young women appeared willing to commit themselves to fight for political causes, which was reason for great concern to many veteran feminists. Many feared that young women believed the war for equality was over—that it had already been won. Few experienced feminists, such as Steinem, doubted that there would be more battles in the future. But would there be enough committed women to rally behind feminist causes?

During Gloria Steinem's lifetime, great progress has undeniably been made. Women in the United States face far fewer instances of open discrimination and prejudice than in the past. Today, economic and political power is more accessible to women than it has ever been. A greater percentage of American women have obtained positions of influence in government than ever before. But some feminists have argued that there is a darker reality behind the apparent signs of progress: More women are working simply because they have to, out of economic necessity.

This fact is tied to a frightening trend that has been referred to as the "feminization of poverty." During the 1980s, more and more single mothers entered the ranks of the working poor; and many working-class women, unable to benefit from the opportunities available to middle- and upper-class women, have seen an erosion of their status as well.

Equally significant has been the challenge to the right to reproductive freedom, long cherished by feminists. Through public policies and, more importantly, Supreme Court appointments, the Republican administrations of

Ronald Reagan and George Bush have aggressively rolled back many publicly mandated abortion benefits, although they have been unable to overturn *Roe* v. *Wade,* the 1973 Supreme Court decision guaranteeing the right to an abortion.

The outlook for feminism is thus mixed. Feminists can point to such successes as the elimination of widespread stereotyping and legal discrimination. Yet there have been setbacks as well, such as the failure of the ERA. Despite the advances of past decades, there are still many battles to fight, such as the struggle for reproductive rights, equal pay for equal work, and child care legislation.

The record of Gloria Steinem's achievements is an impressive one. She once said that early in her involvement with feminism she thought it would occupy only a few years of her life, and that she would soon return to her "real" life. But it wasn't long before the movement itself became Steinem's real life. For her, as for millions of women, the discovery of feminism—that "first candle in the dark"—illuminated a new meaning and a new vision of life.

Important Events in Gloria Steinem's Life

1934	Born March 25 in Toledo, Ohio.
1956	Graduates *magna cum laude* from Smith College, with a major in government.
1956-58	Studies at the universities of Delhi and Calcutta.
1960	Moves to New York City and takes a job with *Help!* magazine.
1968	Begins writing a political column for *New York* magazine; writes first openly feminist article, "After Black Power, Women's Liberation."
1971	Produces the first edition of *Ms.* magazine. Helps found the National Women's Political Caucus.
1977	Helps organize the first National Women's Conference in Houston, Texas. Awarded a Woodrow Wilson Scholarship to study feminism.
1978	Helps organize the Women's March on Washington.
1983	*Outrageous Acts and Everyday Rebellions* is published.
1986	*Marilyn*, a biography of the movie star Marilyn Monroe, is published.
1987	*Ms.* magazine is sold to John Fairfax, Ltd., an Australian media firm.
1990	*Ms.* magazine reappears as an independent, reader-supported journal devoted to feminist issues.

Notes

Chapter 2

1 Gloria Steinem, *Outrageous Acts and Everyday Rebellions* (New York: Holt, Rinehart & Winston, 1983), p. 130.

2 Steinem, pp. 131-32.

Chapter 3

1 Steinem, p. 135.

Chapter 4

1 *Current Biography,* March, 1988, p. 47.

Chapter 5

1 Steinem, p. 16.

2 *Current Biography,* Thirty-Third Annual Cumulation (New York: H. H. Wilson, 1972), p. 413.

3 Steinem, pp. 241-42.

4 *Current Biography,* Thirty-Third Annual Cumulation, p. 412.

Chapter 6

1 "Gloria Steinem: A Liberated Woman Despite Beauty, Chic and Success," *Newsweek,* August 16, 1971, p. 52.

2 Gloria Steinem, "After Black Power, Women's Liberation," *New York,* April 7, 1969, p. 8.

Chapter 7

1 Steinem, p. 18.

2 Steinem, p. 19.

3 Steinem, p. 20.

4 Steinem, p. 113.

5 Steinem, pp. 117-18.

Chapter 8

1 Steinem, p. 111.

2 Marilyn Mercer, "Gloria: The Unhidden Persuader," *McCall's,* January, 1972, p. 68.

3 Mercer, p. 68.

4 Mercer, p. 125.

5 Vivian Gornick, *Essays in Feminism* (New York: Harper and Row, 1978), pp. 151-52.

6 "Steinem at 50: Gloria in Excelsis," *Newsweek,* June 4, 1984, p. 27.

Chapter 9

1 Steinem, pp. 290-91.

Chapter 10

1 Steinem, pp. 328-29.

2 Steinem, p. 131.

3 Steinem, p. 146.

Chapter 11

1 *Current Biography,* March, 1988, p. 49.

2 *Newsweek,* June 4, 1984, p. 27.

3 *Newsweek,* June 4, 1984, p. 27.

4 *Current Biography,* March, 1988, p. 50.

Suggested Reading

Berger, Gilda. *Women, Work and Wages*. New York: Franklin Watts, 1986.

Henry, Sondra, and Emily Taitz. *One Woman's Power: A Biography of Gloria Steinem*. Minneapolis: Dillon Press, 1987.

Hinding, Andrea, ed. *Feminism: Opposing Viewpoints*. St. Paul: Greenhaven, 1986.

Morgan, Robin, ed. *Sisterhood Is Powerful: An Anthology of Writings from the Women's Liberation Movement*. New York: Random House, 1970.

Steinem, Gloria. *Outrageous Acts and Everyday Rebellions*. New York: Holt, Rinehard & Winston, 1983.

Steinem, Gloria. *Marilyn: Norma Jeane*. New York: New American Library, 1988.

Whitney, Sharon, and Tom Raynor. *Women in Politics*. New York: Franklin Watts, 1986.

Index